PRAISES FOR

HOW I OWN CEREBRAL PALSY

Carmen is both beautiful and intelligent. The determination she has to conquer her dreams is inspirational. This book allows readers to step into her fabulous world. It is a must read for those looking for insight and motivation to reach their own aspirations.

~Jacqueline

Carmen is an absolute inspiration! Wise beyond her years, her story will humble and inspire you, bring you to tears and make you laugh.

~Luis

Carmen is such an inspirational young lady. Her insight has motivated me to never give up on my own dreams. Despite her Cerebral Palsy, she continues to fight for what she wants in this life with a smile on her face.

~Francis

It brings joy to my heart to know that my niece, Carmen has accomplished one of her dreams. Her determination to write such a moving book, which educates the world on Cerebral Palsy in such a personal way, shows the strength of her character and the love in her heart that will only encourage her readers further.

~ Yvette

Carmen is not only my beautiful friend, she is the rainbow in everyone's cloud. I am so proud of you and this amazing story you are about to release

~ Talena

Carmen, brings light and joy to my life. I am blessed to have a granddaughter who is unique and loving. This book will allow you to understand what love, family, friends ethnicity means to her.

~Doris

Carmen is not only an amazing person, she has a gift. The gift of life and love. This book was written with her heart in her hand. When you read it you will understand

~Daisy & Kenny

Carmen is my first born niece. She has shown me that anything is possible. I am so proud of her and I know that the sky's the limit when it comes to what she is capable of. Despite her disability she has the power to change the world. I love you Cai

~Carlos

I am very proud of my Carmen, not only is she amazingly beautiful and smart, but she can light up a room with her contagious smile. I know she can and will achieve anything she puts her mind to. I love you more than words can say.

~ Titi Carmen

HOW I OWN CEREBRAL PALSY

CARMEN LEBRON

13TH & JOAN
2018

Printed in the United States of America.

First Printing, 2017.

Copyright|2017 by Carmen Lebron

All rights reserved. No part of this publication may be reproduced, distributed, or transmitted in any form or by any means, including photocopying, recording, or other electronic or mechanical methods, without the prior written permission of the publisher, except in the case of brief quotations embodied in critical reviews and certain other noncommercial uses permitted by copyright law. For permission requests, write to the publisher, addressed "Attention: Permissions Coordinator," at the address below.

13th & Joan

500 N. Michigan Avenue, Suite #600

Chicago, IL 60611

WWW.13THANDJOAN.COM

DEDICATION

I dedicate this book to all my beautiful differently-abled people who have dreams and don't know how to reach them. Just go for it and let God guide you all the way. Look at me and how far I have come. My dreams are becoming reality.

ACKNOWLEDGEMENTS

To my parents (Jacqueline & Luis). Thank you for always being there and providing me with unconditional love and support. I am a blessed young lady. Mom, thank you for standing by me and inspiring me as I wrote this book, and for the constant love, which goes beyond words. Daddy, you are my rock. Our bond is like no other. Your hugs and kisses are cherished within my heart. You're my world.

To my God, thank you for never abandoning me. Thank you for guiding me throughout this awesome journey and for instilling this gift in my heart. Without you nothing is possible. I love God!

A very special thank you to Patricia Carrozzini, for an amazing photo for the cover of this book.

In order to understand me and the world I live in, you must sit in my wheelchair for a day. Then you will see life for what it is. It will be the experience of a lifetime, which you will never forget.

PREFACE

I recognized over my years of living that we all face trials and tribulations. What I have learned is that we possess the power to overcome any obstacle that is placed before us. For me, some may see Cerebral Palsy as a disability. I have never been disabled. I have only channeled the power that is inside of me. I know that the world needs this same power. This book is purposed to help readers discover their power.

INTRODUCTION
Accepting Life for What It Is

When I started journaling it was mainly for me to vent. I never imagined that it would be a book today. My life is mine and I am proud of it. People have this assumption, because I am in a wheelchair my life is miserable. On the contrary it is beautiful and a blessing. I am just as normal as the person who is able-body. I have my struggles just as you do, except I handle them differently. I love myself for being me and I love you for you

TABLE OF CONTENTS

CHAPTER 1. How I Own Cerebral Palsy 1
CHAPTER 2. Surgeries and Love 5
CHAPTER 3. Dealing with Cerebral Palsy ... 15
CHAPTER 4. Religious Girl 19
CHAPTER 5. Being Boricua 23
CHAPTER 6. Missing my Titi Yvette 29
CHAPTER 7. Extra Hands in My Home 35
CHAPTER 8. Insomnia 41
CHAPTER 9. Daddy's Little Girl 49
CHAPTER 10. Party Girl 51
CHAPTER 11. My Birthday Years.............. 55
CHAPTER 12. Moving Out..................... 61
CHAPTER 13. Miss New Jersey 67
CHAPTER 14. I Only Have One Mother 73
Epilogue 77
Carmen's Challenge 79
About the Author 87

CHAPTER 1
How I Own Cerebral Palsy

Hello, I am Carmen Aurora Lebron. I am 18 years old and I have Cerebral Palsy. Cerebral palsy (CP) is a group of disorders that affects muscle movement and coordination. It is a disability among children, which is caused by damage to the brain at birth or during the pregnancy. The word "cerebral" means having to do with the brain. The word "palsy" means weakness or problems with the body's movement. There is no cure for CP, and it is not something you can catch or inherit. I am fortunate to have only a mild case of Cerebral Palsy. For me, the disorder prevents me from being able to walk and do many of the everyday things most people take for granted.

The reason I chose to write this book is because I want to get the word out on what Cerebral Palsy is and how the disorder doesn't have to run your life. My disability and wheelchair don't define me, and nothing can stop me from achieving my dreams. I will become the first super model in a wheelchair. The person I was brought up to be is the definition of Carmen. I'm a happy and energetic girl who loves to go out and stay out late. I don't need your pity because my parents raised me to be strong and to never feel sorry for myself. I look forward, never back.

My parents divorced when I was three years old. I have the coolest and cutest dad in the world. I love him because he never abandoned me like so many of the kids without dad's. I live with my dad every other weekend the bond that we share is like no other in the world. We speak at least five times a day. I can talk to him for hours, and there is never a boring or serious moment between us. He is, quite simply, one of the funniest people I know. I am and will always be Daddy's little girl.

My mother is the strongest person I know, and she raised me to be strong like her. She is a beautiful light-skinned queen who takes care of me in the best way. She makes me work hard for what I want in life and reminds me, that just because I'm in a wheelchair doesn't mean that I can't succeed in life. She is my rock and I am hers. In addition, my mom makes sure that I look amazing from my head down to my toes every day. She keeps my wardrobe up to date and fabulous. She is the most amazing woman and I love her to the moon and back.

So, although my parents are divorced, they get along well, which I am thankful for. My dad comes to my home to visit whenever I ask him to. They are just cool friends and together they have the best intentions for me.

Reflections

What is something that you have had to overcome in your life?

_____
_____
_____
_____
_____

Who has inspired you?

_____
_____
_____
_____
_____

What are your challenges today?

_____
_____
_____
_____
_____

CHAPTER 2
Surgery's and Love

In 2009 I had my first hip and thigh surgery. Before surgery, I wore a hip brace all day long that was designed to keep my hips and legs from rotating inward. The brace was made out of metal with belts of cloth. I hated every minute I had to wear it and I cried and begged my mom to not put it on me. My mother, however, knew it was for the best. My only break from the contraption was before bed and I looked forward to every evening when she would take it off. I knew she was doing everything she was told in order to avoid me having surgery. For five years we went through the same routine and it was not easy for my mom. Each morning she got me dressed and put the hip brace on. Then, she would carry me to my wheelchair, so we could both continue with our days.

I had to visit my orthopedic doctor every six months. On the day of one particular appointment, I had a feeling that my visit was going to be different. It started out completely normal. We signed in and waited to be called. I then received a hip x-ray and waited while the doctor reviewed it. The wait seemed longer than usual and when the doctor came in, I knew that something wasn't right. The x-ray, which Dr. Therrien placed on the light box, showed my hip bones dislocating from the socket. He explained to my parents that it was time for surgery and since I was still growing he recommended fusing the hips before they completely dislocated.

After hearing the doctor's plans, my mother came over to me and hugged me. Her tears made puddles on my face. I was so scared, nervous, and just wanted to leave. My dad took me out of my wheelchair and hugged me so tight. I could feel his heart throbbing against mine. I cried on his shoulder and held him right back.

On the way home, my dad kept saying everything was going to be fine, but somehow that just didn't make things better. The weekend following my appointment came and went. My mom had to schedule the surgery with my doctor's office, but she didn't tell me when it would be. Sometimes, being kept in the dark is a good thing. It allowed me to focus on my life without worrying about the future, even if it was only for a little while. On October 29, 2009 my mom decided to celebrate Halloween early. I had no clue why and thought it was a fun idea. She dressed me as a Raggedy Ann doll and we took pictures at home. I remember her filling up my pumpkin basket with lots of candy and I probably should have known then that something was up. It wasn't till later that night, right before bed, that she told me the reason we'd celebrated early. Mom carried me to the sofa and sat next to me. She explained that I was scheduled to have surgery the next day. I started to cry as my mind went into worry mode and my mom moved me onto her lap and cuddled me as I soaked her pajama shirt with my tears. We were both a mess! Surgery is a scary word for anyone, but if we would have known more about God, we would have been stronger. I say that because when you have faith in your heart and know that God is the center of your life, you'll never face fear alone again.

Since my mother already knew the date of the surgery, she had packed a duffle bag for the both of us because we were expected to stay in the hospital for seven days. After we arrived at the hospital and I was all checked in and prepped for surgery, my dad carried me into the operating room. I remember holding him tightly as he laid me down on the cold table. I was so scared to be left alone and continued to hold his hand as the anesthesiologist placed the mask over my nose and mouth and I fell asleep. The surgery was no walk in the park. It lasted more than six hours, but at least I was asleep for that part. It was my rest before the storm, because let me tell you, after surgery, that was when things got real. After coming out of surgery I remember being in the recovery room. The hospital only allowed two visitors at a time to see me. My Titi's, Carmen and Rosa were there and though I could barely open my eyes, I heard there voices clearly. I was happy that they remained throughout the surgery to make sure everything turned out well. Later on, after I was moved into a private room and the effects of the anesthesia wore off, I was in so much pain that the doctors had me on morphine. I could hear my mom crying because she couldn't do anything to stop or help me with the pain. One thing I remember my mom doing was laying beside me and singing me our favorite song, "You Are My Sunshine." She sang to me all night, with a knot in her throat, trying to hold back the tears. She felt broken and useless seeing me in such agony, so singing to me made her feel like she was helping in some way.

My dad would pace back and forth, not knowing what to do for me. I remember him yelling out in the hospital hallway for someone to come and help stop the pain. As the days went by, my entire family came to visit. It was like a very quiet party with no music. My pain was unbearable so they kept things calm and peaceful.

After six days in the hospital, I went home to continue my recovery. It took me six months to recover. My mom and dad would take turns monitoring me and caring for me. Because of their love and the support from the rest of my family, I am certain that I recovered faster. My bedroom was like a revolving door with visitors in and out every day.

Sadly, during my recovery, I learned my hospital time wasn't over. During surgery my doctor had put metal plates on the sides of my thighs to keep them from rotating inward. So, when I noticed the stitches on the side of my thighs, I asked my parents what they for. They explained it all to me and how I had to return for more surgery to remove the plates. By that point, I was tired of being scared. I decided it was time for a positive change in my attitude. I'm a strong, young lady and nothing can take me down. I told my parents, "Let's do it." I look at life like this: If it's to better me then why not go for it? I have the best parents in the world. They will do anything to keep me happy, healthy and to see me succeed in life. If this surgery was meant to improve my hips and help me manage my pain, then I was all for it. Today, I have many scars from those surgeries, but they are beautiful, and they tell my story.

In 2012, I was scheduled for a spinal cord fusion surgery. My spine, unlike most, was shaped like the letter C. For two years, prior to surgery, I used a body brace to try and help straighten my spine. I wore it every day, except for when I was sleeping. It was very uncomfortable leaning to one side with my head tilting over. Watching TV was the worst. I was often reminded to pull myself up or my mom would come and physically straighten me in the wheelchair. Despite my best efforts to remain straight, my body would do the opposite. You can only imagine my frustration. Along with the body brace, I also tried physical therapy at home and even at school. I was hoping to prevent any further surgeries to my body, but it was to no avail. My efforts and the efforts of my doctors weren't working, and my last x-ray proved it.

So, there we were again, talking about surgery. When my doctor explained what was going to be done during the procedure, I began to cry. Don't judge me, you would have too. It was harder this time because my daddy was not at the appointment. It was just me, my mom, and my Titi Yvette. I did not have my big strong dad to lift me from my wheelchair and hug me while whispering in my ear that everything was going to be okay. As the doctor continued to give my mother the information to schedule the surgery and what to expect, I saw her soft beautiful face sadden with the news. She came over to me and hugged me tight, our tears began to intertwine. My Titi Yvette tried so very hard to be brave and not cry, but God knows it was impossible. She broke down as well. Just imagine, three females crying in an exam room and the doctor is the only male. He couldn't have flown out of there any quicker. Well the drive back home was like we'd just left a funeral. We were either quite in our thoughts or crying. My Titi Yvette, was the first one to break the silence when she asked me, "Are you okay?"

"I need my dad," was all I could say.

Surgery day came very quickly, as I had only three weeks to prepare myself. My poor mom kept a brave attitude during that time. There was a lot of running around to do before surgery, and I think the busyness helped her get through the days. I had visits to doctors to get my blood work and urine sample done. She made a big production out of preparing my room for when I returned home from the hospital. The room was sanitized, professionally painted, and she bought new sheets for my bed. My mom also made sure to buy herself a sleeping cot which she put in my room because she didn't want to leave my sight. It was a stressful time, but she had everything perfect for when I came home.

The day of my surgery, I remember waking up at three in the morning. My mom carried me to the bathroom and brushed my teeth, washed my body, and arranged my long hair into two braids. It was a silent morning until my Mom put me in my chair and gave me my cell phone to call my dad, who kept me company while she showered and dressed for the day. We had to be at the hospital by seven o'clock in the morning and my dad was at our house by six to pick us up. When we arrived at the hospital, my family was there to wish me luck. From my dad's side, it was my Titi Carmen, Titi Rosa and Tio Flaco. On my mom's side, Titi Yvette, Tio Anthony, grandma, and her boyfriend Junior, as well as my cousins Jailyn and Alexia who came to see me. Yes, my family loves me and the support they gave me, and my parents was awesome.

After a brief visit with my family members it was time for me to head to pre-op. With only my mom and dad by my side, I was prepped with an IV and then wheeled toward the operating room. My mom and dad were only allowed to go with me to the end of the hall and I held my mom's hand the whole way. When it was time to go, I told my mom, "Don't let go."

With tears running down her face, she whispered, "See you soon. I love you." She later told me that removing her hand from mine and walking away felt like she was ripping out a piece of her own heart.

My dad went for a walk during surgery. It was how he dealt with stress and it helped to soothe his thoughts. My mom was comforted by the rest of my family that was there, but she said everyone was in tears and couldn't stop crying.

Six hours later I was in the recovery room and then I was moved to a private room for the remainder of my stay. The pain was unreal, but the drugs were better this time around. After day two, I was able to sit up a little and eat. My mom and dad stayed with me and my family came to visit almost every day. Being in the hospital can take a toll on a person, so when it was time to go home, I was relieved.

Today, I have a perfect spine. Because of surgery and the fusion, my lateral movement is limited, but at least I no longer lean to one side.

Reflections

Have you ever had to have surgery? If yes, explain.

_____
_____
_____
_____
_____

What what your recovery like after surgery?

_____
_____
_____
_____
_____

What limitations did the surgery help you overcome? What limitations do you still have?

_____
_____
_____
_____
_____

CHAPTER 3
Dealing with Cerebral Palsy

Dealing with Cerebral Palsy has its ups and downs, but I never let it get in the way of my happiness. I do my best to live a normal and happy life. Listening to music and dancing to it makes me feel alive. I love to spin in my wheelchair and dance away. Sometimes, I imagine what it would feel like to actually dance in a pair of heels. Maybe one day I will be doing it. For now, I will put on my stilettos and use my wheels to dance away. Just because I'm in a wheelchair doesn't mean that I can't live my life like the average person who can walk. Like I said before, I just have to do things a little different to get it done. I have a fantastic life. I have a mother who loves me unconditionally and would do anything to make me happy. But pity is not an option. I will not be looked at as the poor girl in the wheelchair. I work hard for what I want. You see, I have a story that was already written for me. Now, I'm just living it. My Creator will one day lift me from this wheelchair if he chooses to, and if that doesn't happen then maybe I was meant to be in a wheelchair.

I used to get frustrated and cry when my mom would ask me a question and I did not have the answer quickly enough. It would make me question my intelligence and my disability. Now, I know that If I am asked a question very quickly, it will take my brain time to process the question. Although, I wish I was in control all of the time, my brain and my body just don't get along. I have learned throughout the years that the person in control of my disability is God. I do not look at myself differently. I just might have to do things a few times more to get it right, but trust me, I will get it done. I do not like to give up because God has not given up on me. I have good days and bad days just like you. On my bad days, I cry and get emotional because it's raining outside, or I just heard bad news. Bad news affects me a lot. My good days, however, are all about laughing, writing, listening to music and loving life. I may not be able to walk, run, or jump, but I am able to write, speak, and eat by myself and that is something to be proud of and not taken for granted.

My favorite Tio (Uncle) is a true inspiration. Although Cerebral Palsy is not a condition you can inherit, he, like me, was born with it. Our similar diagnosis has formed a bond between us. He can make me laugh like no one else can and we love to tease each other about football. We banter back and forth about our favorite teams; he loves the 49ers and I am a Jets fan.

It isn't just our laughter that keeps us close. He encourages me to continue fighting for what I want in life. He is a hard working man and I respect him for that. He hasn't let our condition hold him back. Although he can walk, I see his struggles, but his drive for independence only motivates me further. I know he is proud of me, but what he doesn't know is how proud I am of him and how honored I feel to be his niece. I love you Tio.

We all have to deal with something in our lives. Whether it's a disability, toxic relationship, family drama, caring for a sick relative, job issues, the list can go on and on. But all of these issues are dealt with in different ways. Depending on the type of person you are, you either handle the situation well or you don't. My point is, don't give up. Keep trying to become a better, happier you. Don't let anyone drag you down to misery. Getting help or venting to someone is okay. I vent to my dad all the time. He listens to me and then gives me advice. Sometimes we just need someone to just listen.

My mother always tells me that I am perfect just as I am. The truth is, there is nothing I would change about myself. I love myself just as I am. I think I am a phenomenal young woman with a bright future. I know this will not be the end of me, but just the beginning of what life has in store for me.

Reflections

Do you believe your disability will negatively affect how successful you are in life? If yes, explain.

_____
_____
_____
_____
_____

Describe the daily challenges you face and how you overcome them?

_____
_____
_____
_____
_____

When you are having a difficult day, what do you do to change your mood and outlook on life?

_____
_____
_____
_____
_____

CHAPTER 4
Religious Girl

God created me just as I am, and I love him. I don't ever complain about my life, nor do I ever pity myself. I serve a powerful God and serving him is an honor. Because of God, my life is complete.

I was the typical Puerto Rican child raised to follow the Catholic traditions. In other words, I was baptized at the age of one and had a big party, but there was no meaning for me behind it. After my Baptism, my parents and I never attended church. It wasn't that I didn't want to go, but the churches near us were either closed or not wheelchair accessible.

In 2014 my Titi Yvette went back to church, along with my Tio Eddie, and my cousins Jailyn and Alexia. One Sunday, they invited my mom and me to join them. It was all new to me, and when I first entered City Line Church it was overwhelming. The choir came on the stage and started singing about God and before I knew what was happening, I saw people crying left and right. The ones that weren't crying were lifting their arms upward to the sky. I couldn't understand what it meant. I didn't understand their reactions. The songs and the people made me feel so sad, so I tugged at my mom's arm and asked her to take me home. My mom and aunt took me to the back of the church and explained what everything meant. They told me that it's okay to cry and worship to the Lord. God wants us to sing to him and release our pain unto him. As the minutes passed, I began to understand what they meant. It took me some time, but I got it eventually. You have to understand, when something new is introduced to me my brain needs time to adjust and grasp the concept. New events and situations are hard for me at first. So, once I was comfortable, we went back to where my uncle and cousins were sitting and listened to the music. After a time, the Pastor came on stage. When I saw Pastor Joshua for the first time, I felt this calmness come over me. It was as if I had no reason to be sad or worried. When he began to preach, I understood every word and felt an immediate connection. Now, his wife, Pastor Paula, is an angel sent from God himself. Meeting her for the first time was amazing. She hugged me as soon as we were introduced, and it felt as if I'd known her forever. My God is so good to me and He makes sure to put people in my life who respect and genuinely love me.

Today, I love to attend service on Sundays. I love to worship and connect with my God. I drive to the front of the church with my mom and start to sing my heart out. Lifting my arms up as high as I can feels amazing because I know my God is there. "Now faith is the substance of things hoped for, the evidence of things not seen" (Hebrews 11:1, KJV)

Sometimes I feel like I'm about to pop out of my chair from all the worshipping I do. My God is awesome, and He deserves more than worship. With all that God has done for me, I can only thank Him by being faithful to Him. He is my father, protector, and king. I pray every day and talk to Him a lot because I know without Him I would be a lost soul. God has been there for me and never let me down. I am a Christian and so proud to say it. I love my God and will defend Him at all times. Why? Because He is alive. Pastor taught me to live by faith, not by sight. In other words, I do not need to see God in order to believe in Him. My faith in Him is bigger than my sight. "The LORD *is* my strength and my shield; my heart trusted in him, and I am helped: therefore my heart greatly rejoiceth; and with my song will I praise him." (Psalm 28:7, KJV)

REFLECTIONS

1. Do you believe in God? Why or why not?

_____
_____
_____
_____

2. Who do you rely on when life gets hard? God? A family member? A friend?

_____
_____
_____
_____

3. In what way do they help you?

_____
_____
_____
_____

CHAPTER 5
Being Boricua

My parents are Puerto Rican Americans. Yes, they were born in the United States, but my grandparents (mis abuelos) were born on the island. My parents raised me to be proud of my ethnicity and to celebrate and enjoy our heritage. Food is a very important part of our culture and the dishes must be made with love in order to be enjoyed. Some of the more traditional dishes are rice and beans, pork, avocado, and our famous dessert, flan.

My abuela is the best cook in our family. When she cooks for me, it feels like I'm in heaven. The love she puts in the food is like no other and because of her, I have tried many of the Puerto Rican dishes. Just mentioning her cooking makes my mouth water.

Being Puerto Rican is awesome, but being a proud Puerto Rican is even better. My dad had me listening to salsa music since I was three years old. He was raised old school Puerto Rican and salsa is his jam. When I began to understand the beats of the music, I fell in love with it too. If you close your eyes and listen to the musical creations of Victor Manuel, El Gran Combo, Gilberto Santa Rosa, Ismael Miranda, Hector Lavoe, you'll understand where I'm coming from. The combination of the conga, guiro, maracas, and the guitar will make your heart throb. The music sends chills down my spine and gives me goosebumps.

I love my heritage because we are a loud and proud group of people. Que Viva Puerto Rico is one of our famous sayings. My parents taught me to represent my culture and to never deny it. While I celebrate being Puerto Rican every day, there are two days during the year that the celebration of our culture is escalated. During those days there are parades honoring our heritage. One of them is near our house and I am able to attend and participate in the festivities. I was even part of the parade for a couple of years because my dad was the president of the event and I was given the title "Children's Ambassador." It was exciting to represent the children of my town and I enjoyed the responsibilities that came with the title. I was invited to attend the Gala, which was an amazing experience. The event was quite dressy, and I love nothing more than to get dolled up in all of my girly clothes. It was such a treat to have my hair, makeup, and nails professionally done. My father put together a great parade and I couldn't have been prouder of him.

The other parade I mentioned is in New York City. It is known to be one of the largest parades, with nearly two million people attending. My mom tells me that it is a great experience, but with so many people it can be dangerous, so for now, I watch it from the safety of my home. If it was up to me, I would be there every year with my two huge Puerto Rican flags taped to my Wheelchair. I hear the food is great and the after party is even better. Maybe, one day, I will have the experience of seeing it live and in person. Then I will be able to yell out "Wepa," which means "All Right! Good Job!" I can also shout "Boricua," which is the word for Puerto Rican, but my favorite saying to cheer would have to be "Que Viva Puerto Rico," or "Long Live Puerto Rico." and be able to yell out the famous Puerto Rican words: Wepa, Boricua, Que Viva Puerto Rico. Without a doubt, I am so proud of the beautiful island my family comes from and the story it tells.

In general, Puerto Ricans love to party and dance. We can turn any event into a celebration, but my mom and I love birthdays especially. It's the only day to celebrate you and another year of living. No matter what, my entire family gets together on Fridays to have dinner, talk, and laugh. Things can get very loud, with everyone talking over one another, but it is always a great time. Though the living room is large enough to hold everyone, we generally mingle more in the kitchen because we consider it the heart of our home.

My dad is considered very old school and not just because of his taste in music. He is the traditional Puerto Rican Papi and feels that I should never wear makeup and that my first boyfriend should be when I'm thirty years old. I love my dad and I'm glad he protects me and treats me like his princess.

Having cerebral palsy doesn't mean I can't still live my life. I love being a fabulous Puerto Rican girl, and I'm going to live this life to the fullest.

Reflections

How has your nationality and cultural background influenced your life and upbringing?

_____
_____
_____
_____
_____

Do you feel like certain cultures are more accepting of the disabled?

_____
_____
_____
_____
_____

What do you love about your own culture and/or heritage?

_____
_____
_____
_____
_____

CHAPTER 6
Missing My Titi Yvette

Bad news is never good news. It was a Saturday morning and my mom was about to transfer me from the bed to my wheelchair, so I could use the bathroom, when I noticed her face was looking kind of sad. It was as if something was on her mind. I said, "What's wrong mommy? Are you going to cry?"

She said, "We have to talk. It's about your Titi Yvette."

Now, let me tell you about my Titi. She is one of those people that is beautiful both inside and out. She is tall, with a head full of beautiful curls, and a body shaped like a guitar. Her smile is one of a kind, as she has deep dimples in her cheeks and when she hugs you, she can bring warmth to your heart. Beyond that, she is always dressed superbly, and the added touch of perfume completes her perfectly.

Titi Yvette and I became extremely close because in 2010 she became my one to one aide in school. She is my one and only assistant within the building. Originally, I had an aide assigned to me by the school, but she was not following my care plan. A lot of the help I need involves personal care. At school, that means that I need someone to assist me when I need to use the bathroom. When I am on the toilet, I need a harness to keep me secure as I cannot sit up without assistance. The harness is designed to fit across my chest and ties over my shoulders and around my waist. It provides me support while also allowing me the privacy of using the restroom stall alone. Without the harness, I'll lose my balance and inevitably injure myself, which is exactly what happened with the original aid the school provided me. She placed me on the toilet and did not secure me with the harness. I was young at that time and didn't notice before she left me in the stall. As expected, I lost my balance. I fell forward and though I tried hard to keep myself in place by holding onto my pants, it didn't work. I went crashing down to the restroom floor, hitting the wall with my body. It was a hard fall because I don't have the ability to protect myself. The banging of my body hitting the floor, along with my crying in pain alarmed the aide. She came into the stall and immediately started to panic. Not knowing what else to do, she picked me up and rushed me to the nurse's office. At that time, Titi Yvette was working in the Physical therapy department as a secretary. She saw the aide running with me in her arms down the hallway. By this time, I was crying so loud that my Titi became very upset and finally took me in her arms to comfort me. She let me know that my mom was on her way. Thankfully, she was studying to become a teacher and the University was across the street from my school. Titi Yvette held me tight till my mom and dad arrived. Later, at the doctor's office, my injuries were assessed and while the right side of my face was very red, tender, and swollen, I was actually very lucky because my glasses had protected my eye socket from breaking. Needless to say, the aide the school provided was dismissed and Titi Yvette was asked to step in and take care of me during school hours. I can't tell you how grateful I was for her care that day.

So, when my mom told me that morning that she needed to speak with me about Titi, I felt my stomach drop. It turned out that my beautiful, loving, patient Titi Yvette was leaving me to start a new job. To hear those words from my mom's mouth felt like someone was squeezing my heart. It hurt to know that the one person I trusted at my school was leaving me. My brain was in STOP mode. I cried so much and could not concentrate for days. I wondered who would care for me while I was at school? Who could I trust? Would the next aide be as good, patient, caring, and responsible as my Titi Yvette? Oh my God. What was happening and why did she want to leave me? These were my questions to my mom every day. I felt robbed. It was as if I was never going to see Titi again. Change is a huge problem for me as I have trouble accepting it. It takes me time to understand why things are going to change.

As time went by and Titi Yvette's last day drew closer, she and I would speak about the upcoming changes. Each day I would ask her why she needed a new job and each day she would explain that she had a family to support and the new job was going to provide better pay and opportunity. She made it clear that she would always be my Titi Yvette and the change had nothing whatsoever to do with me. The bond we shared was special and she loved me like I was her own daughter.

I began to understand as my mom and dad explained to me what she meant. As the time drew closer to her last day, I made sure to cherish every hug and kiss from her. I tried to make the best out of every minute, second, and hour I had with her as my aide. Before she resigned, she recommended another person she knew from my school who would make a good one to one aide for me. Wanda was trained directly by my Titi Yvette and she does a good job with me and I appreciate her very much.

Today, Titi Yvette and I still have a very close relationship. We see each other as often as we can and speak via the phone or FaceTime when we can't see each other in person. I know she would be here for me in a heartbeat if I needed her. When things go wrong or I'm having a bad day she immediately calls me. She reminds me to pray or takes the time to pray with me on the phone. It's still not the same as seeing her every day at school, but I've come to realize that as long as Titi Yvette is happy where she works, then I'm happy for her. She even went back to school to further her education and I am very proud of her. She is a great mom to my cousins and an awesome wife. Titi Yvette is the aunt that every young girl wishes she had.

Reflections

Where does your favorite Titi (aunt) or other relative live? Why are they your favorite?

_____
_____
_____
_____
_____

How has your Titi (aunt) or other family member motivated you?

_____
_____
_____
_____
_____

Have you ever expressed to your favorite family member the influence they have had on your life. If yes, what did you say and how did they react? If no, then write what you'd like to say to them below.

_____
_____
_____
_____
_____

CHAPTER 7
MY HOME

In 2004, my mom noticed we could use a little help with carrying me to the bathroom and transfers around the house. We were blessed that it was my Titi Carmen. Yes, I have many aunts. She became my first home health aide and the first person my mother ever trusted and left me alone with. It was good for my mom because she did not have to miss classes at the Community College, or rush from running errands to meet me at the house before the bus dropped me off. My mom did it all for me, but in order for her to finish college and earn her Associate's degree she needed some help. My Titi Carmen was sweet and for two years she cared for me like her own daughter.

After Titi Carmen resigned, we hired a great loving home health aide. She was older, but so strong and it helped that I was smaller then and light as a feather.

Since she spoke only Spanish, I began to understand the language even more. She would sing to me and I would repeat the words. Bath time with her was especially fun as she would teach me Spanish and I would try to teach her English. We spent a lot of time laughing. She stayed on as my home health aide for three years. She would have stayed longer, but after leaving my home one day she had an accident. She was at her house, up on a ladder trying to install new curtains, when she lost her balance and fell on top of the window air conditioner. She was rushed to the hospital and needed surgery on her right hand because the fall had cracked her wrist. Her injury and recovery meant she could no longer work as my home aide.

At this point, my home became a revolving door of home health aides. My mom is very serious and particular about who she trusts with me. The agency would send home health aides to my home with little to no knowledge of what my condition was or how to help me. My mom was forced to be very strategic and thorough during the interviews. The questions were real and serious. Have you ever cared for a child with special needs? How patient are you? Do you know how to clean a bathroom? Do you know what Cerebral Palsy means? Do you have a good grip and how is your back?

Their experience and strength determined their opportunity to work with me. If the interview went well my mom would offer them the job on a two-week probation period. My mother didn't play around with my health or my safety. She would train the home health aide herself and never left me alone with them unless she really trusted them. You have to understand, it wasn't only my condition that made her so cautious, I am also her only child.

It took years to find another good home health aide. I feel that in order to work in that field you have to love what you do. You must enjoy working with people and want to help them. This is not a job for the weak, or someone who's only interested in flexible hours and easy money. My mom and I didn't want or need someone who was lazy or someone who was going to love me. I already had people to love me. What we wanted was someone competent and capable of taking care of me. You see, I need someone who is able to lift me because I can't be dropped, and I can't risk falling, and while I can stand, by holding on to another person, I still need assistance with many things in my daily life. The point is that I am not a cute doll to play with, to dress up, and rearrange. I am a human being.

In addition to my mom's school schedule, she also needed help because she wasn't feeling as strong as she had been. My mom began to feel weakness in her hands and arms and because she didn't want to drop me, she made the decision to hire some help. As the years went by, my mom's condition worsened, but she never gave in. She refused to stop caring for me and wanted the majority of the responsibilities on her shoulders.

Over the years, we have gone through at least fourteen home health aides. There were a variety of reasons as to why these applicants didn't work out. Some of them didn't see the need to work because they saw my mom as a young, fit, and strong mother who shouldn't have needed any help. They didn't understand she was fighting through her weakness and visiting as many specialists as she could to figure out what was wrong with her body. Others took advantage of her kindness and would ask her to get them food and coffee while they were on the clock. Another would come late and leave before she was supposed to. There was even one who fell asleep on the sofa all the time. My mother did not expect them to become my nanny, but she did expect their help and dedication to the job and me. After all, it was hard for my mom to allow strangers to enter our home, but she did so because we both needed the help. Thankfully, my Titi Yvette was willing and able to help us when we were between hired aides.

As of today, I am happy with my home health aide. Francis is the bomb.com and I have nothing but love and respect for her. She has been with us for two years and is very sweet, patient, funny, and most importantly extremely helpful. She loves her work and it shows. Her ability to care for me is wonderful and it helps my mom a lot. Francis is a fantastic mother of two little girls, and

I think that has helped her in understanding how to best take care of me. She has never questioned my mother about her weakness and even on her days off, will come and help me if I need her to. That is dedication.

Reflections

Can a stranger become a part of your family?

_____
_____
_____
_____

What attributes do you require in a home health aide or any assistant you hire? What skills do you find most important?

_____
_____
_____
_____

What interview questions would you have for a home health aide or other assistant, whether it is for you or another family member?

_____
_____
_____
_____

CHAPTER 8
INSOMNIA

In 2009 I was lucky enough to visit Jamaica with my mother and grandmother. We spent eight days on the beautiful island and had the most fantastic time. When we came back from the island, my mother purchased a new bedroom set for herself. Normally, I would have been happy my mother was doing something for herself; she deserved that new furniture and so much more. From the age of three till eighteen, I slept in the same bed as my mother. There was something so comforting about her bed and I always slept well, however, everything changed when she received the new bedroom set.

The first night in the new bed went fine, but every day following seemed worse and worse. I would fall asleep at nine o'clock and be awake again by ten. For years this same pattern continued. I slept for only an hour or two every night. It was so frustrating and my supportive family tried everything to help me. My mother would cuddle me or place me on her chest to comfort me. My father would come and see me in the middle of the night when I called him crying with exhaustion. Nothing seemed to help. My brain was wide awake. Eventually, my parents brought me to a psychologist who recommended testing, but everything came back normal. With no other options, I was prescribed three types of sleeping pills, none of which helped me.

Everyone was frustrated, tired, sad, and overwhelmed, especially my mom who dealt with my sleeplessness on a nightly basis. The issues eventually carried over to the weekends I spent at my dad's house. Even if he held me, I could not sleep. Many nights, regardless of whose house I was at, I stayed up watching television. Thankfully, I had so much energy, that I was still able to attend school, but my parents were not so lucky. They were drained. My mother eventually accepted the fact that I had insomnia and did research to get a better handle the situation.

Today, I am healthy and am able to get to sleep and stay asleep through the night in my own bed in my own room. I would love to tell you that we figured out what the trouble was, but the truth is that the sleeplessness eventually went away on its own. Maybe it way all the praying and crying, but whatever the reason, I am glad those rough four years are over.

Reflections

Have you ever had trouble sleeping
and do you know the cause?

_____
_____
_____
_____
_____

Do you have trouble falling asleep,
staying asleep or both?

_____
_____
_____
_____
_____

Have you seen a doctor? Did medication
or some other remedy help you?

_____
_____
_____
_____
_____

How did lack of sleep affect your everyday life and what, if anything, did you do to compensate for it?

_____
_____
_____
_____
_____

How did it affect your relationships?

_____
_____
_____
_____
_____

CHAPTER 9
Daddy's Little Girl

He is mine and I will forever be daddy's little girl. We have this bond like no other and I love him to eternity. He is my safety zone and I know that nothing bad could ever happen to me while he is around. Just picture this 6'1", dark skin, handsome, diesel Puerto Rican man and you'll understand that no one in their right mind would ever try to test him. I'm his only daughter and though I am not his only child, our connection is unbreakable.

We speak on the phone at least five times a day and connect through Facetime often. I like to check and make sure he's eaten and taking care of himself. When I speak to him, a smile spreads from ear to ear on my face. Since my mom and dad's divorce, I spend every other weekend with my dad and he comes to visit me every Thursday.

When I go to my dad's house, I look forward to seeing my little brother, Macho's and is cheerful face. He is my energy bunny and I love to see how excited he gets when I come to his house. He runs down the stairs and greets me with hugs and kisses. Although he is much younger than me, Macho loves and cares for me in a way that I will cherish forever. If I drop my spoon or my phone he will get it for me. There was a time when I choked on my food and Macho came over to me to make sure that I was okay. The concern on his face was adorable. We like to watch movies together and Talena, my dad's wife, moves me to the reclining sofa and has Macho sit beside me in my wheelchair. For him, my wheelchair is a novelty.

We are a united family and I love and appreciate how Talena and Macho receives me. Talena is a wonderful wife, mother, and best friend. She cares for me like I'm her biological daughter and always reminds me that I can do anything I put my mind to. I love her dearly.

Do you ever feel like something is missing in your life? To me, that's my daddy. I wish our time together never ended. It never feels like enough and I'm hoping that one day I will be able to live with him. Yes, I am thankful that I get to speak with him every day and I know that compared to some girls, who don't even know who their dads are, I am blessed. I am grateful to God that he has allowed my dad to still be part of my life and that he chooses to want to see me. My dad has been to every specialist appointment from infancy. He has been there for every surgery that I have had to endure, and never left my side. When I get sick with a cold or the flu he rushes to my rescue. Don't get me wrong my mom is an angel and takes care of me the majority of the time, but when my dad comes to see me, he becomes my medicine that makes me feel better.

Our father, daughter relationship is a blessing. I could never be upset with my dad, and he has never been upset with me. When he's having a bad day, he calls me to cheer him up and I give him the best advice I can.

He is my world and protector and I know that God is by his side. I have a great deal of respect for my dad and I aim to please him because it is important to me that I make him proud. He tells me all the time that I am a LeBron and there's nothing I can't do. You see, giving up is not in our blood. We have to try hard and if we fall, we have to get back up and try harder the next time. My dad doesn't look at me as his poor daughter in a wheelchair. He treats me like he treats my brothers.

I pray to God that He continues to help guide my daddy on every decision he had to make and to continue giving him strength, so he can keep caring for me. I have his back throughout this journey called life and I hope one day to repay my father for all that he does for me. When he is old, I'd like to care for him and spoil him the way he has cared and spoiled me. Perhaps, someday we will travel the world and go on grand adventures. No matter what, I love you Daddy and I will forever be your little girl.

Reflections

Do you have a father figure or other role model in your life?

_____
_____
_____
_____
_____

Explain your relationship and how they have influenced your life?

_____
_____
_____
_____
_____

Because of their influence, do you find yourself wanting to mentor others?

_____
_____
_____
_____
_____

CHAPTER 10
Party Girl

I love to party! I love when the music plays loud, and I can feel the vibrations from the ground up through my body. The feeling of music makes me happy and sometimes I feel like I'm about to pop out of my wheelchair. The truth is, I could be having the worst day ever, but when I play my music it's a wrap. I start smiling and laughing as if my day was never ruined. Music is therapy and brings life to the soul.

I love being invited to weddings, sweet 16's, and birthdays. I enjoy the excitement and seeing my family and friends. There is nothing better than good food and dancing. And let me tell you, I was born to dance. Last summer I went to a wedding with my mom and the DJ was great! I knew every song he played, and I kept wiggling my body from side to side to the beats of the music. Listen, I have moves like no other and I can out-dance and outlast anyone on the dance floor. I don't get tired, my feet don't get sore, my shoes always look brand new, and I certainly don't get winded. I own my cerebral palsy and the wheelchair that gets me around. I can turn and spin like every able-bodied person, only I do it better because my turns are controlled.

Because I am only seventeen years old, I have never been to a club, but I would like to see what all the hype is about. My cousins and friends tell me about their experiences and all of the loud music and different flashing colored lights. My mom tells me that I have to be careful if I ever decide to go to a club because of the alcohol and how certain people act. I guess for now, to be on the safe side, I will party from my home, but once I'm twenty-one, I'm planning on going. Trying new things can be good and bad, scary, and fun, but how will I ever know if I don't push myself to try.

When I dance I feel like I'm on "Dancing with the Stars." To be on that show is one of my dreams and I know it will come true one day. This world is becoming more and more accepting of people with disabilities, so my chances of being a participant isn't so far-fetched.

When I went to that wedding last summer, a gentleman approached my mom and asked her permission to dance with me. My mom leaned forward and asked me if I wanted to and I nodded yes. It was my first time agreeing to dance with a man who was not my father or another family member. It was new and very exciting, and I knew my smile had spread from ear to ear. He said hello and I believe he told me his name, but the music was too loud to hear him clearly. We danced to a Merengue song and I was shocked that he was keeping up and not getting tired. It was a fast-paced Spanish song and some of them can last up to eight minutes. I guess he loves music as I do. It was wonderful to be asked to dance and it made the night even more special. I'll say this though, if my dad had been at the wedding, I would probably be telling you a completely different story.

Reflections

What brings joy into your everyday life?
Music? Art? Food?

_____
_____
_____
_____
_____

Do you find your interests therapeutic? How so? .

_____
_____
_____
_____
_____

Is there an interest you have that
you have not pursued?

_____
_____
_____
_____
_____

CHAPTER 11
My Birthday Years

I just cannot believe that I'm now eighteen years old. It feels like I just celebrated my seventeenth birthday yesterday. My mother tried to surprise me with a cowgirl party at the park, but the weather was terrible. There was a thunderstorm and it got worse each minute. I had no clue that the party we were going to was my own, but I did know that my mom was panicking. She started to cry and began to pace back and forth while talking on the house phone. She also kept opening the door to look at the sky and assess the weather.

I couldn't take her sadness any longer. It broke my heart to see her that way. So, I asked her what was going on and why she was crying? Mom began to explain to me how she and my dad had planned a huge surprise party for my birthday, but due to the weather she either had to cancel it, or relocate it. At that moment, I was so emotional. While my parents have always celebrated my birthday, it had never been a surprise. We decided to move the party to my Titi Yvette's house, so my mom wouldn't lose all the money she'd invested in my celebration. I was sad that the weather had ruined my surprise. She'd even hired a party planner to decorate the park pavilion. Because of the weather, a lot of people did not show up. We had food for days and my cake was fabulous. Despite the weather, everything turned out great.

Even though my dad couldn't make it to my party, and I was sad he wasn't there, he still managed to hire a caricature artist to draw people during my event. Thankfully, I was able to celebrate with him on the actual day of my birthday. He took me to an awesome Hibachi restaurant and I ate like a beast. It was a beautiful place and we had the table for ourselves.

Since I was one year old, my parents have celebrated my birthdays in a big way. It has always been with a two or three-layer cake, lots of food, and lots of family and friends. My mom loves to throw birthday parties. She tells me that it is the only day you get to feel extra special and it's another year God has given us to live; so, why not celebrate it and make it loud and fun. I agree with her.

My Sweet 16 was the best party of my life. My parents went all out. I had no limit on money and whatever I wanted they got it. I did not go the traditional route, with the court and limousine. I wanted the party to be about me. My dress was made in California. It was white with ostrich feathers and when I tell you I looked incredible, I mean it. I had my makeup and hair professionally done before the event. The venue was to die for. My parents had rented the Fiesta and it was amazing. I had a photographer and videographer to capture each moment. The theme I chose was masquerade and everyone had a mask on their seats when they entered the room. My parents made their grand entrance, then my brothers and my dad's wife, Talena, followed. Once they were in the room, the DJ asked everyone to stand because I was making my grand entrance. The doors opened, and I rolled in, full of excitement and with the biggest smile ever. I immediately felt this rush of energy running through me. Everyone was clapping and taking pictures with their phones. Now, it was time for the changing of my shoes. My dad removed my flat shoes to put on my first pair of high heels. Next my parents gave a speech about me. It was beautiful. My mom choked up and my dad was a mess. He cried because he couldn't believe how much time had flown by and how far I'd come in my life. It was very touching.

After the speech, I had my first dance with my dad and it was a moment I will remember forever. We danced a Spanish Merengue song and then he lifted me out of my wheelchair and hugged me as we continued our dance to John Legends song, "All of Me." I kept giving him kisses on his cheek and squeezing him tight because I did not want to let him go. It was my day and I just wanted to freeze that moment. The song lasted a few minutes, but at the end when he dipped me everyone went crazy, yelling and crying because he did it so gracefully. It was the best birthday party ever. All my family was there, and we were able to take pictures, eat, and dance the night away together. It was definitely a night to remember.

Reflections

If you had to choose one person to celebrate your birthday with, who would it be?

_____
_____
_____
_____
_____

Describe one of your birthday wishes.
Did it come true?

_____
_____
_____
_____
_____

Describe your ideal birthday celebration.

_____
_____
_____
_____

CHAPTER 12
Moving Out

Have you ever lived somewhere for a long time? Well, I have. I lived at 395 Virginia Avenue for twelve years. It was our first apartment after living with my Abuela for two years. My mom searched for a long time for that apartment and worked hard to get it for us. I thought Virginia Ave was my forever home, but our time there came to an end.

That first apartment was a cozy two bedroom on the ground floor, which made it wheelchair accessible for me. It was part of a three-family house and we had private parking for our large conversion van. The van has a ramp installed in it, so I could drive my wheelchair right up. The apartment also had a little back yard that my mom bought a grill and patio set for. Every spring, she would clean the yard and get the grill ready. We would have breakfast, lunch, and dinner outside until the weather changed, and it became too cold to stay out there that long.

Since I upgrade my wheelchair every five years and it just gets bigger and heavier each time, it really became a problem. As the years went by my mom noticed my wheelchair wasn't able to fit through the bedroom or bathroom doors. So, she had to park the wheelchair by the bedroom door and carry me into the individual rooms. I was not able to go to the kitchen so while I was in the wheelchair I was basically confined to the small living room for much of the twelve years we lived there. Eventually, my mom began looking for a bigger place for us because we really needed the extra room.

After searching for a bigger place, my mom found the right one and told me that we were moving. Lord only knows how hard that news was for me. Although I knew Virginia Avenue was getting tight, I loved it there and it took me some time to accept the news that we were leaving there soon. My mother started calling moving companies before I even had a chance to see the new place.

After a few weeks we went to see the apartment. It had a parking lot and a ramp for my wheelchair. The apartment itself was located on the second floor and when we entered and looked around, I started to feel sick to my stomach. The apartment was beautiful and so big, and I saw the excitement on my mother's face, but all I felt was sad. For me, our home was still on Virginia Avenue. My abuela was with us and she noticed that I was upset so she took me outside for some fresh air. Don't get me wrong, it was a nice place with huge bedrooms and a spacious living room, but I was so used to my old apartment that the new one wasn't impressive to me. Regardless, the move needed to happen, and I had to let Virginia Avenue go.

Moving day came so quickly and my mom was elated to get us out of our cramped space. The moving company loaded our belongings into the truck and just like that we were out. I was shocked at how fast an apartment can look so empty and cold after leaving. There was no congregation of neighbors to wish us farewell when we left. We had not made a lot of friends on Virginia Avenue. My mom didn't like to make friends with neighbors. She would say hello or good night when we would see them, but never invited anyone to our BBQ yard parties or into our home. Mom felt that our lives should be kept private. Those who did come to visit were only family and close friends.

The drive to the new apartment was nerve-racking. My mom ended up having to pull over to talk with me. Even though the move had been in the works for a while, I needed to hear the explanation one more time. She explained to me again that the new apartment was going to be great and how I was going to be able to pick out new furniture with her. She let me know that the new place would feel strange for a little while, but that eventually it would feel like home. I looked into my mom's eyes and noticed they were watery, as if she wanted to cry. I asked her why she was sad, and she said, "I'm not sad, these are happy tears." I knew better though. I could tell that she was just as sad and scared as I was. Neither of us like change, but we know it is a part of life.

Today, we live in the new huge apartment and I am happy. I picked out my new bedroom furniture and my mom decorated the other rooms. She was right; it did eventually feel like home. I still miss Virginia Avenue though, and from time to time my mom takes me past our old place when we are out for a drive, so I can see it.

Reflections

Have you ever had to move? If so, why?

_____
_____
_____
_____

How did you feel after the move?

_____
_____
_____
_____

What adjustments did you have to make when you moved?

_____
_____
_____
_____

CHAPTER 13

Miss New Jersey

In 2015, I ran for Miss New Jersey and it was the best experience. My mother signed me up online and I was interviewed by several judges to see if I had the qualifications. At the time we had no idea what we had gotten ourselves into. Within a few weeks we received an acceptance letter and to celebrate, we went shopping for dresses and outfits.

We learned that the competition was held over a three-day period, from Friday to Sunday morning. My mother booked a room at the hotel where the event was being held and then asked my Titi Yvette and cousins Jailyn, Alexia to stay with us. Just getting ready for the competition was a lot of work. My mother and Titi were my glam squad and they made sure to style my hair and makeup differently for each event. I had five different outfits because I wanted to compete for several different titles.

When we first arrived at the hotel on Thursday evening, we unpacked and went to register. I was so excited to start the competition and to meet all the other girls who were going to compete. Registration was like a seminar. My mom had to pay for every competition I signed up for and we had to listen for instructions and read all the documents right then and there in order to sign in.

My mother takes everything very seriously when it comes to me. She would never just sign her name on the dotted line. She read and asked twenty questions before she signed any of the documents and she needed to know who the person in charge of the show was and whether they were aware of my wheelchair. Although she had made sure to ask that question before signing me up, sometimes people forget. The day of registration my mom made it her business to let those people running the pageant know that she needed to see the ramp that would bring me to the stage. She wanted me to be able to practice using it. My mom is no joke and she doesn't leave anything to chance and I love her for that. She knows how to have fun, but when it comes to me, she takes control so there will be no accidents.

Thankfully the people in charge knew of me and my wheelchair situation and they made sure to make me feel comfortable. Being part of the pageant was a good experience. It gave me the chance to see that I can try out for almost anything in the world. I might have to do things a little different, but I will get it done.

I was in competition for two whole days with only a three-hour break. I competed for Most Photogenic, Best Casual Dresser, and Best Spokesmodel. Competing with the other girls was fun. Some of them had been competing for years and it was second nature for them. As for me it was all new and an experience I will never forget.

In the end, I was one of the top fifteen running for the title of Miss New Jersey. When I heard my name, I was in shock. It felt like my wheelchair was stuck to the ground, but it was me. I froze and couldn't move. I thought for sure that I had misheard them, and I looked for my mom in the audience to assure me that I had heard correctly and should head out on stage. Before I even moved, my mom came back stage and hugged me. She was in tears and leaned forward to say: "My love, this is big. You're one of the top fifteen runners. I am so proud of you. Remember, whether you win or not, I want you to take this experience and know that nothing can stop you from succeeding in life. I love you, Baby."

I took her words, turned my wheelchair, and drove up to the stage with the attitude of a diva. When I looked out to the audience, I saw my beautiful family. There they were supporting me again. My Titi Carmen, Talena, Dad, Macho, Grandma, her boyfriend Junior, Titi Yvette and my cousins. Just seeing them there made my crazy nerves go away.

I told myself that if I won that would be great, but if I didn't at least I could say I tried. I didn't end up winning, but in my heart, I did. I may not have left with a crown on my head, but the overall experience was worth more to me than the crown.

Reflections

Have you ever dreamed of being in a pageant? Why or why not?

_____
_____
_____
_____
_____

What are your dreams and aspirations?

_____
_____
_____
_____
_____

Being in the pageant required my being on stage in front of many people? Is public speaking something you are fearful of?

_____
_____
_____
_____
_____

CHAPTER 14
I Only Have One Mother

My mother is a strong Latina with an even stronger personality. She is the woman who will give you her last ten dollars, and also take care of you until you are back up on your feet again. However, don't ever take advantage of her because when she gets hurt or upset, that beautiful heart of hers goes out the window. My mom has done it all for me and continues to love and care for me on her own, because love has no price.

Monday through Friday, my mom wakes up at six in the morning to get me ready for school. She carries me to the bathroom and helps me clean myself up for the day, then carries me back to my room to get dressed. Once she places me into my wheelchair and fastens my seatbelt, she allows me to choose my own accessories while she makes me a hot breakfast. I have never eaten a cold breakfast in my life because my mother spoils me every morning with eggs, bacon, hash browns, toast, and a glass of water.

The way in which my mom takes care of me and loves me is amazing. She tells me it is an honor to be my mom, but I know it has been challenging for her at times, not only because of my condition, but also because being a single mother is hard work. We have had good times and bad times just like everyone else, but the good times far outweigh the bad moments we've shared. She loves music and to dance. I learned my moves from her. We have vacationed together, and I've never heard her once complain about caring for me. I say all this because caring for me and herself can be a lot. I worry about my mom every day. After all the specialists, her diagnosis was discovered, and it turned out she has a muscle disease. It's been a couple of years now, but in the beginning, it was quite a surprise and has been a journey to accept. Today, she is stable and still takes care of me, but she has a little help. She wants to care for me alone, but her muscle disease doesn't allow her to. She has told me how much it hurts her to not be able to do it all by herself. My mom is a fighter and she pushes herself to take care of me until she's exhausted her body. I know there are days that she can't lift me, but somehow, she still gets up and takes care of me. The love and respect I have for my mom is indescribable.

We are given one mother, so it is my duty to take care of her as much as she takes care of me. I make sure to call her when I'm in school to check in and see that she is ok. I make sure that she has eaten and taken care of herself. When I leave for my dad's house, I call her regularly, not only to check on her, but because I miss her a lot when I'm away. She is hilarious and cracks me up. She is such a jokester.

Our bond is like no other. We go out a lot and it's never a dull moment with her. Because of my mom, I get to see the world. So far, I have been to Florida, Jamaica, the Dominican Republic and on a Cruise.

My mother is the most beautiful women I have ever seen. I don't say it because she is my mom; she really is beautiful. She has long dark brown hair, with big brown eyes and a smile that can stop anyone. When she hugs me, I always hug her a little bit longer because she smells just like a mommy should. Her aroma is a mixture of cotton candy, flowers, chocolate, and cake batter. But more than anything else, her heart is her best asset. She has an incredible ability to love and isn't shy about sharing it. Each day she tells me that she loves me, and I will always appreciate and love her back. I owe her so much. It is because of her that I am who I am today. She instilled confidence, bravery, wisdom, and beauty in me. In order for me to write this book I had to build confidence and pray that I was capable to do it. Because of my mom and her love and support, I was able to write my journey.

REFLECTIONS

Describe your mother's parenting style? Is she strict? More of a friend? Or a bit of both?

_____
_____
_____
_____

Describe your mother in one word?

_____
_____
_____
_____

If you could repay your mother for all that she has done for you, how would you do so?

_____
_____
_____
_____

EPILOGUE

I want the world to know that just because you have a disability it should not stop you from becoming that teacher, lawyer, author, doctor, etc. It's important for people to understand that I have a voice. My wheelchair does not define me. I will change the world, one person at a time. "How?" you ask. By explaining and educating them about me and my Cerebral Palsy.

You are not powerless. You are powerful beyond measure and I challenge you to do the work to discover your greatest power.

CARMEN'S 5 DAYS OF GRATITUDE CHALLENGE

For the next five days, I want you to reflect upon what you are grateful for and how you can make a difference in the world, just as you are. Use the space below to write your answers and to reflect.

Day 1:

What are you grateful for?

_____
_____
_____
_____
_____
_____
_____

How did you make a difference today?

_____
_____
_____
_____
_____
_____
_____

Day II:

What are you grateful for?

_____
_____
_____
_____
_____
_____
_____

How did you make a difference today?

_____
_____
_____
_____
_____
_____
_____

Day III:

What are you grateful for?

_____
_____
_____
_____
_____
_____
_____

How did you make a difference today?

_____
_____
_____
_____
_____
_____
_____

Day IV:

What are you grateful for?

_____
_____
_____
_____
_____
_____

How did you make a difference today?

_____
_____
_____
_____
_____
_____

Day V:

What are you grateful for?

_____
_____
_____
_____
_____
_____
_____

How did you make a difference today?

_____
_____
_____
_____
_____
_____
_____

Far too often, we don't do all that we can to make a difference because we think that we are not perfect or that we don't have the power. Nothing could be further from the truth. We can make a difference right where we are. Taking time to reflect upon what we are grateful for and how we can be impactful is an act of great power. This pattern of thinking can make all the difference and help us to take action. I challenge you to take action to make someone smile, to encourage those around you and most importantly, to love everyone. That's the true definition of owning your life, your way.

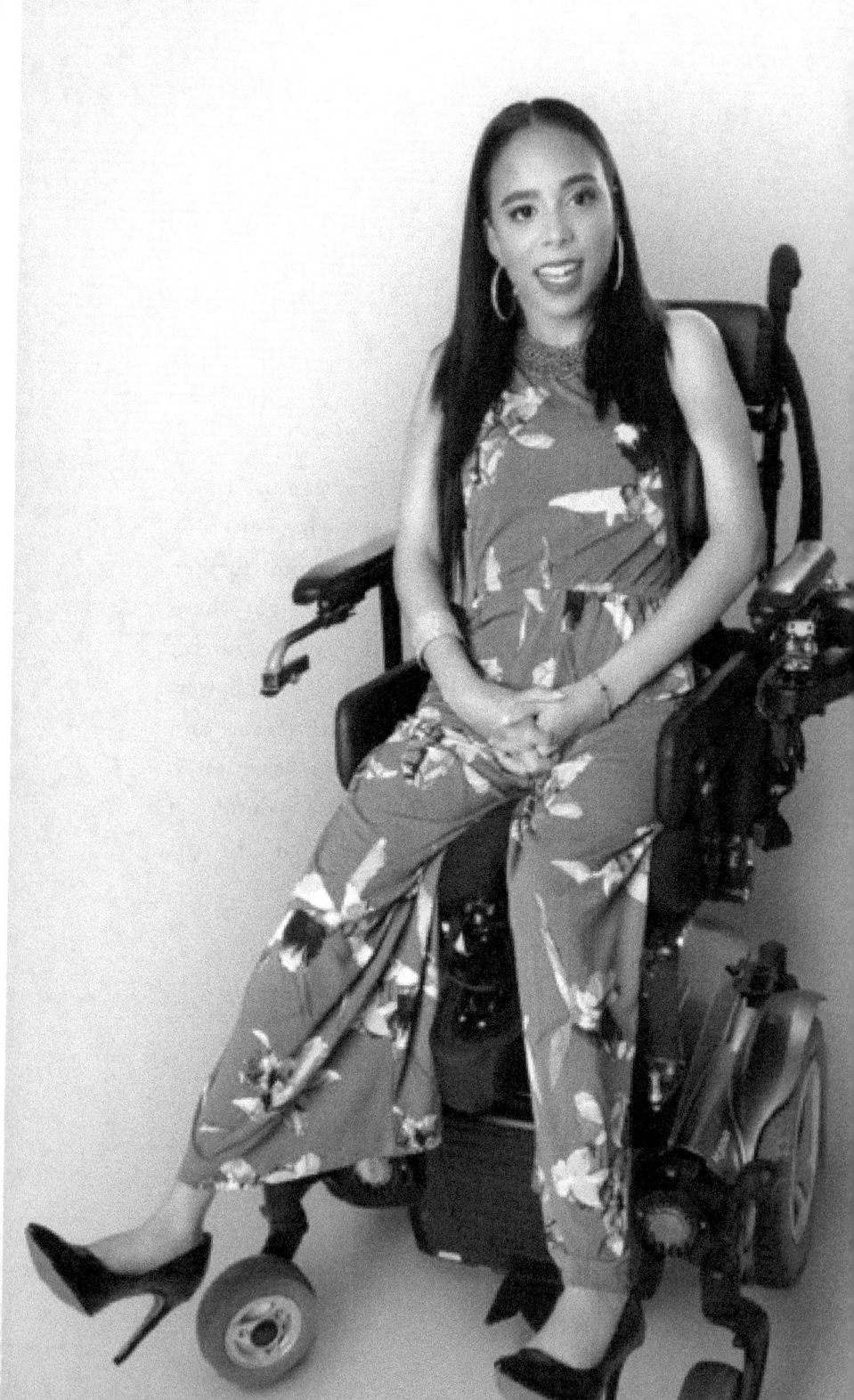

ABOUT THE AUTHOR

Carmen Aurora Lebron was born on September 21, 1998, in Jersey City, New Jersey, to Puerto Rican parents, Jacqueline and Luis. She has an older brother, Luis Jr, and a younger brother, Luis Lebron. In 2015 Carmen competed for Miss New Jersey and was one of the top 15 finalist. It was the best experience for her. Additionally, she was the children's ambassador of Puerto Rican Parade for two years. Today, Carmen is a senior in high school where she is the president of the KeyClub. She has also recently graduated from the modeling school, Barbizon. She hopes to one day become a model and actress.

CONNECT WITH CARMEN

Website: www.authorcarmenlebron.com
Instagram: @mswheelchairmodel

www.ingramcontent.com/pod-product-compliance
Lightning Source LLC
Chambersburg PA
CBHW050440010526
44118CB00013B/1620